T0354787

I DO . . . BUT TO WHO?!

LINGEELA JOHNSON

authorHOUSE®

AuthorHouse™
1663 Liberty Drive
Bloomington, IN 47403
www.authorhouse.com
Phone: 1 (800) 839-8640

Published by AuthorHouse   01/15/2018

ISBN: 978-1-5246-9040-3 (sc)
ISBN: 978-1-5462-2513-3 (e)

Print information available on the last page.

This book is printed on acid-free paper.

CONTENTS

2009

2010

2011

2012

ACKNOWLEDGEMENTS

First, I give honor to my Lord and Personal Savior, Jesus Christ. It is a privilege to give you glory because that is what I was created for. This book is a form of worship, and I give that back to you. I can do nothing without you, but all things through you that strengthens me. Next, I give thanks to the Baxter, Cooper, Bryant, and extended families. This book is dedicated to my favorite girl, my mother, Betty Jean Johnson. I could never repay you. My debt to you is how I live my life. Availe, I LOVE YOU. YOU ARE NOT ALONE. I AM PROUD TO BE YOUR BROTHER. I AM SO PROUD OF YOU. I NEVER HAVE TO BE SAD BECAUSE MAMA IS ALIVE THROUGH YOU! To my father, Pastor Donnell Johnson and his beautiful wife Cheryl… thank you for all that you have done and for your FAITHFULNESS TO GOD!

To Lorraine Williams and Prophetess Deborah Walker, I don't have the words to say, but I can say, thank you and I LOVE YOU!!!

To the Fairlawn Baptist Church, where it ALL started and the foundation was laid. Thanks to the entire church family. I want to personally thank those precious souls who now are resting in peace: Mother Viola Bell, Deacon Silas Harden, Mother Margaret Bing, Brother James Gordon, Cousin Lucille Edwards, Deacon Rufus Peters, and Mother Bernice Peters. I also want to thank Minister Denise Miller, Minister Kevin Simmons, the Fairlawn Male Chorus, Deacon Michael and Sister Betty Grant, Deacon Thomas "Bo" Simmons, Mr. Elliot "Booster" Simmons, Mother Sophie Simmons, Mrs. Grace Simmons, Sister Earlyn Simmons, Mrs. Bertha Gibbons, Mrs. Geraldine Mobley, the entire Sunday School staff, Minister Denise Miller, Minister Kevin and Holly Simmons, Brother Marion Bryant, and Coach Bakari Bryant. To Avon and Bettina, Tre, Trent, Tristan, Emanuel and Andrea, Lil Man, Justin, Eden, Chris and Nakashia ("*The Girl of My Dreams*"), Andrea, Precious, *Girls For Jesus*, Amp and Tab, Imani, Nigel, Jalen, Tyler, Ayana and Kelan, Keita, Ms. Rela, Jonathan Williams, (Mama Clara), Jobina, John Jones, TeLisa, and

Chartavia, I appreciate you. To my hometown of Savannah, Georgia and Garden City, thank you for making me proud of where I was reared. To R.W. Groves High School where I started and A.E. Beach High c/o 1995 where I finished, as well as every school in the Seaport City of Savannah, I salute you. Mrs. Claire, Angie, Salon 360, Pure Perfection, Brown Sugar, GI The Hair Doctor, Marquita, Jovan, Tyrek, Vanessa, Brandon, Charles, Eric "Scissor" Hines, Mark Ervin, Pastor Terry Alexander, Cornerstone Salon, Devalon, Omar, Keith, Keith, Keenan, Corey, The Clique at Beach High. RIP to everyone that passed away in the Class of 1995 @ A.E. Beach High School.

To Pastor William Green Jr., you helped me grow during those formative years. You took the time with our youth department, and you never despised our youth. You understood and listened as a man placed in a precarious position of leadership. Thank you and First Lady Robin Green for your encouragement and opening up your door during the Dallas Cowboys' glory years in the early 90s.

To Pastor Harold Edwards, Minister Emanuel Gray, and Minister Victor Logan at Fairlawn Baptist Church, preach the word in and out of season. Thank you Pastor Edwards for being a man of integrity who has a HEART for the people of God. Thank you Mama Sandra for your love, support, and encouragement. Thanks to Pastor Zion (CCL) and Pastor Anthony Edwards at Beulah Baptist Church-- real men of God with integrity. Let's work.

To Bishop Wade S. McCrae, your transparency was the hammer that broke the rock into pieces during my collegiate days at Valdosta State University. I am humbled that you consider me as one of your favorite people. Thank you for your interaction as well as giving me a platform to recite one of my psalms. Bless you and the entire Union Cathedral family. To Phi Beta Sigma Fraternity, Incorporated and Zeta Phi Beta Sorority, Incorporated and the entire Spring '98 Line. Blue Phi and Z Phi! To all my brothers and sisters in other fraternities and sororities at VSU, Red and Black... All Hail Special! Shout out to Jacqueline Harris and Dani Ross who were my sounding board and help.

To the Prayer Team at Cathedral of Faith, you all taught me the value of prayer and faith in Christ.

To Pastor Creflo and Taffi Dollar at WCCI, your simplistic teaching has empowered me and given me the experience of witnessing ministry on a global scale. Minister Gwen Thompson and the Singles Ministry, I'm grateful to you for allowing me to recite my psalms in order to share my gifts, as well as teaching me how to experience victorious single living.

To MY Pastor, Gary Monroe, YOU ARE AWESOME…let's transform the City and do it for the Homestead and for ALL the residents of Garden City. Deacon Tony Johnson, Deacon James Horry, Papa Joe Ford, Mother Cotton Ford, and the ENTIRE FORD FAMILY, RIP to Mr. Willie Monroe Sr., Mr. Buggy, and Mrs. Claudette!

To Pastor Demetrics Scott, Pastor Yolanda C. Scott, New Life, and the ENTIRE INTERCESSORY PRAYER TEAM (Monday-Friday @ 7 am EST, (302)202-1104, CODE 486458, PLEASE MUTE YOUR PHONE!!!

Thanks to Pastor Betty Byrd and The Lord's House For All People!!! Pastor Eddie and Cheryl Armstrong, Pastor Willie Feagins, RIP Apostle Rose. Andrew and Walter Family YMCA on Campbellton Road and the entire staff.

To Elder Turner, Evangelist Elizabeth "Mama" Turner, Auntie Ula, Rod, Antonio, Shawn, Kat, Josh, Lil CJ, and the Redeemer's House Family, I LOVE YOU TO LIFE. You cannot fathom the impact that you have on my life. You two are a dynamic duo operating in the power of one for the Kingdom of God.

"UNBREAKABLE 2: THE SERIES" (STAY TUNED . . . THERE'S MORE TO SEE)

We interrupt our regularly scheduled program for a new broadcast
Due to irreconcilable differences, the current show has been canceled
There's a new production in the works that possibly could star you and me
To my surprise, I heard that you were looking for a new co-star
I've been interested for quite some time
I was questioning if I would be chosen as a regular or an extra
The director fired you because he said that you were creating a hostile
      environment,
And that you were difficult to get along with
However, the new Executive Producer recognizes your true value, and is
      looking to
Do a new thing from the old television show
Even though you thought you played only a small role in the last season of
      episodes, you attracted the attention from the Owner of the television
      network
I have to be honest; the last man that you hooked up with was only interested
      in the love scenes,
Only wanted to be seen with you on the red carpet, and refused to commit to
      anything long term
I know that you are a serious actress, but nevertheless, you can't stand drama
But from the looks of your male counterpart, the show was a sitcom
He always was "out to lunch, when it came to serious topics such as love,
Commitment, and building for the future
The only reason that he was put on is because the director wanted to use him
      for himself
Not to mention the other cast members
And to add insult to injury, the other ladies around town, who played his love
      interest,
Says that he is known for having a lot of "technical difficulties" . . . plus there's
      nothing to see
I would love to audition for the new role; I bring much more charisma to the
      script

GOD is the Sole Owner, Proprietor, Chairman, and CEO of the entire television network

HIS SON JESUS is the Executive Producer with all the freedom to control the entire set,

Including all cast members

The HOLY SPIRIT is the Director, leading and guiding ev'ry situation,

And editing the bloopers that we make for all the "Days of Our Lives"

You see, you are a virtuous woman, fired because the cast members are employed by the devil

He enjoyed them, owned their rights, and has all the rights for creative control

You didn't last because you began to question the script, and the terms of your contract that were in fine print

However, the best thing that will happen in our lives will be the new reality show that GOD has designed for us

This reality show was thought about before there was even a television.

Not to mention, before we were in our mother's womb

The show stars you and me

There will be a pilot episode to see if we have the chemistry like Ossie Davis and Ruby Dee

There will be no love scenes until the owner reviews my contract of accepting HIS SON, then counseling me about my purpose and commitment to you being the only star in our show

This will be a family-based series that will touch everyone that stays tuned to us,

As we stay tuned to the Executive Producer

My goal for this spin-off: to get us inducted into the Hollywood Walk of Fame

Where I hear the sidewalks are paved with gold

But only if you say "YES" to your new lifetime partner . . .

STAY TUNED . . . THERE'S MORE TO SEE . . . UNBREAKABLE 2: THE SERIES . . . COMING TO A STATION NEAR YOU!!!

I was living in East Point, Georgia at the time I wrote this short story. Alicia Keys had just come out with her single, "Unbreakable," and she inspired me. I was working out on the treadmill at the Andrew Walter Young YMCA on Campelton Road in Southwest Atlanta (SWAT) when I observed the song making an appearance on BET'S 106 and Park. I had no intention or any premonition about writing anything, but I heard the words echoing when I woke up that Saturday morning. They were downloading at a feverish pace as I rushed to find a pen and paper. I would keep them within arm's reach while sleeping, just in case any words or melodies gave me a visitation during the night watches. I wrote at a Usain Bolt sprinter's pace, not being the least bit concerned with structure. Sometimes when you're in the flow, structure and arrangement come later. Needless to say, after all was written, a masterpiece was created on paper to the reader's eyes as of now. Alicia Keys doesn't know it, but she has a remix to "Unbreakable." I was excited about penning this particular work, which was totally different from I was used to creating. I likened this to a movie script and wanted the reader to envision all of the major actors and actresses in their roles with a spiritual twist. The one lead that will never change is that not only is JESUS the light of the world, but He is the star of the show! Because it was already spoken (Rhema Word), it is written (logos): Jesus' part can never be written out. He was not killed. He laid down His life (oxymoron). Jesus was broken for us so that we could be "Unbreakable."

"GOD'S FAVOR"

I'm at the point of no return when I look into your eyes
Though you're not here, when you're away, the love we have stays on my mind
The sun rises and sets when I am near you
Bein' in love looked bleak to me, 'til fallin' for you has given me a clear view
It's been a lifetime plus eternity, since my heart has received good news
Now my song is a beautiful ballad instead of singing the lonesome blues
My arms are much stronger now that you are inside them
Our relationship will have no ending, and this proposal symbolizes the
    beginning
At times, I can be indecisive, but the one thing that I'm sure about is you
And to show and prove that I am certain, this ring will proclaim that "I DO"
I have a hit out on me, but the mafia cannot get me to stay away
Since I can't afford your virtue, I placed your love in the Layaway
I'm forever attracted to the sweet fragrance of your beauty
When I was stuck in the rewind of my past, you're the only *Lady In My Life* that
    moved me
You're the love mechanic that gave me a tune-up, when love broke down on me
Harriet Tubman has nothing on you, because you're the emancipator that
    broke the chains to set me free
Just when I thought my life was over, and my joy was trapped in the lost and
    found
You came along and like Diana Ross, and turned my whole world "Upside
    Down"
When the stakes were high, you arrested my heart, by throwing your cards on
    the table
Though I didn't do anything to deserve *God's Leading Lady*, I was just blessed
    with . . .
GOD'S FAVOR!

The greatest reward that a man could receive is the favor of God extended unto him. God grants man favor when he leads a MAN to find a WIFE (woman Genesis 2:24). A single man only receives a certain degree of favor before getting married. However, when he gets married, he receives the full measure. Men, if you desire favor, I recommend you to get married. The only security in being a bachelor is to care for the things of the Lord. Some are eunuchs, like the cupbearers, some are called to be single like the Apostle Paul, but Mr. Lingeela La'Isa Johnson is not only called to be, but desires to be married! Make no bones or mistakes about it. When a faithful man marries a Proverbs 31 Woman, he cannot be stopped in fulfilling his assignment. God's favor through his wife provokes the man unto good works complete his assignment. A lady is a man's glory and the best gift God created for a man. The greatest covenant partners for a man are the Holy Ghost and a woman. The Bible declares that it is not good or beneficial for a man to be alone. God made Adam a help meet or a suitable, proper fit for him. A woman was fashioned for a man and tailored to suit his needs. A woman knows a man because she came out of him. It is very important for a man never to abuse anything that comes out of him because he only hurts himself (Ephesians 5: 22-23). Men should never abuse, misuse, or degrade the woman that has come to do him good all the days of her life. For the woman is the crown that sits upon his head (Ephesians 12:4). If she is a crown, then he is royalty, first class, regal, and refined. He is a king and kings do not think, speak, or live as paupers. A king shows off his crown. Since the woman's greatest attribute is her hair, she spends the most time and money on it. She takes care of her crown so that she can be his crown (Revelation)! In closing, there is nothing more exciting than for God to join a man and a woman in Holy Matrimony! God grants men favor by making a help meet for him in Holy Matrimony, and we do God a favor by producing glory for him as godly seed. *God's Favor* is coming soon to men everywhere!

"YOUR MATE WILL BE ADDED UNTO YOU"

God must really like me because He sent me you
Although I haven't experienced the rapture, I was "caught up" the first time I
    saw you
When the angelic roll was announced, you answered "present" when it was called
And Cinderella has nothing on you since you were born to ball
Oh yes, you're of a different breed, because dignity and class you exude
You never take the scripture out of context, you allow God's man to find you
You're the topic of every man's conversation, but not for what you do in bed
I know that you're an independent woman, but you're submission always
    honors your head
No need to look in the dictionary because your character is so defining
You never have to wear a watch, to be a part of God's perfect timing
When it's payday, you're never controlling because you make more money
    than me
You understand true education is being trained by the Holy Ghost and not the
    number of certifications, trainings, or degrees
You mean far more to me than what man sees on the surface
With the natural eye, you have flaws, but it is your spirit that makes you perfect
Divine purpose has connected us to carry out heaven's plan
The Savior has sent me a virtuous woman, and delivered you a God-
    fearing man
Nowadays, couples are getting married just to get a divorce
Dating that focuses on sex instead of commitment, is like putting the cart
    before the horse
Never marry to avoid loneliness, seek God before you say "I Do"
If you delight thyself in the Lord while single...................

YOUR MATE WILL BE ADDED UNTO YOU!!!

This was special to me because of the fact that God woke me up at 1:50 am for me to receive something so great. God loves us so much that He will go through the great length of disturbing your rest to communicate with Him. *The Successful Family*, written by Dr. Creflo Dollar, inspired me to write this psalm. I learned the definition of single means to be unique and whole. There is a difference between being alone and lonely. While attending a Single's Conference at Atlanta Metropolitan Cathedral, the Pastor, Bishop Flynn Johnson replied, "Being alone is a spiritual condition that can only be healed by God; being lonely is a physical phenomenon. Once you are healed of loneliness, then you are ready to be joined to a mate." *Your Mate Will Be Added Unto You* signifies that your mate is the icing on your cake to sweeten your life. When you are healed, restored, and delivered of past hurts, then the addition of your mate is inevitable. God is not only the greatest mathematician that adds to your life, but also the greatest matchmaker of all time! A woman should not place her value in how many promotions, certifications, diplomas, or degrees she may have. Her value is that she fears the Lord, her husband trusts her, and her children arise and call her blessed! It is not the stylish clothes she wears, but that she is clothed with the glory of God, how she puts on the whole armor of God, and how she puts on the garment of compassion, the bowels of mercy, and how she is clothed with humility. Call me Babyface, because she's *My Kinda Girl*! The hour has come for men and women alike to prepare their mind, soul, and spirit to position themselves in the Divine timing of God. Then and only then, will your mate be added unto you!

"WHEN WE COME TOGETHER, WE TOUCH AND AGREE"

I said, "I Do," the very first time you said "Hello"

Dazed and confused, refusing to receive God's gift, cause all I felt was the *Love Below*

My last relationships had me goin' round-and-round like a ferris wheel

But when I stopped to hear what my heart was sayin', it said that you're that deal

Before heaven sent you to me, I was tired of being in love by myself

I should have taken heed to the Surgeon General, my last situation was bad for my health

Once upon a time, I thought that pain would be my final destination

But you paved the way to happily-ever-after, you are my confirmation, and our marriage is the consummation

I've never met a lady quite like you, with so much elegance, grace, and charm

Ever since I got rid of unforgiveness, I got so much love inside these arms

My house is not a home, until you foreclose it with your presence

Since we are equally yoked, when we come together and "Slow Dance," we'll be *Steppin' Into Heaven*

My heart has received a transplant, and when I'm near you, it skips a beat

My old address had me living on Heartbreak Boulevard, till you moved me to Love Street

Your personality is brighter than a million light bulbs, in fact, you outshine the sun

Since I left my mother and father, I'll cleave to you, now you have become number one

Heaven has mixed us together a perfect chemistry, for the entire world to see

I'm so thankful God evicted one of his angels and delivered you to me

Because spiritually...........

WHEN WE COME TOGETHER, WE TOUCH AND AGREE!!!

The greatest agreement is for a husband and wife to come together, touch, and agree. Heaven smiles when man and wife are on one accord and connected spiritually. In Holy Matrimony, they already are on the road to becoming one, however, what accelerates the process, is the glory of God, and the power of agreement. Spiritual and emotional agreements are the prerequisites for intimacy, not sex. Sexual intercourse is the dessert to the main course meal of, LTD (love, tenderness, and devotion). Intimacy starts in every room, but ends in the bedroom. We have the irrational thoughts of intimacy beginning in the bedroom. Both men and women need security, understanding: As Mr. Gary Byrd stated, *"Help Me Understand So I Can be Understood,"* effectual communication, and emotional presence. Some guys are here, but not present. When the teacher calls the roll in class, some of the students respond by saying, "Here." Others reply by saying, "Present." In relationships, we are here, but not present! As men, we are here for the woman physically to provide her with a warm body, but we are not present spiritually, emotionally, or psychologically! We need to drastically improve in these critical areas. On the contrary, ladies need to realize that we as men, need to be encouraged, and taught by you. Music Soulchild has a song entitled, *Teach Me How To Love.* He soulfully belts out, "Teach me how to love you, show me the way to surrender my heart (girl I'm lost); teach me how to love, teach me how to get my emotions (E+ energy in motion) involved. This, in my opinion, is one of the most informative love songs of all time. If you listen, I'm sure you will agree. The power of agreement takes effectual communication and like the great Allen Iverson said during an interview . . . "PRACTICE." As Gary Byrd stated, **PRACTICE** means: *P*utting *R*ight *A*ctions *C*hoices *I*nto *C*onsciousness *E*veryday!!!

"A KINGDOM MARRIAGE"

I'm so elated that I made you my selection

I know that the human personality is flawed, however with you, it's impossible for God to improve on perfection

You are the woman I desire to be with, and the only woman, I don't want to live without

Your faith has moved into my heart's residence and has evicted all of my doubts

Heaven has lent me one of its angels, to spend the rest of my life with until the rapture

Consequently, I'm already caught up, because every beat of My Heart you've captured

We go together like Easter eggs and the white rabbit

People will start callin' you Bugs, because in your ring there are so many carats

Like a mechanic, you restored my heart, when love broke down on me

As a result, when God spoke to me concerning you, my spirit quickly agreed

Dear Ms. Beloved, nothing sounds sweeter than you changing your last name to mine

Since you are the undisputed champion who won my love, you are *The Greatest of All Time*

You are the author who wrote the *Book of Love* making history

Because the Holy Spirit teaches you all things, nothing is a mystery

I wouldn't replace you with anyone else

Even when it's that time of the month, you still remain at your best

For better or worse, with you, I'll go through the wire

When your soul is involved, I'll come rescue you, even from hell's fire

The world admires our chemistry, which makes our relationship better than average

People who put themselves together have a wedding, but only God can ordain what we have:

A KINGDOM MARRIAGE!!!

For what God has joined together, let no man put asunder. God endorses Holy Matrimony. God endorses marriage. There is nothing more exciting to God than for Him to join a man and a woman. When a man and a woman are joined, it glorifies God. Not all marriages are joined by God. The first miracle that Jesus performed was at a wedding. Jesus turned water into wine. Wine represents celebration and Kingdom Marriage represents God's stamp of approval. I was inspired to write this soul-stirrer because there were so many people getting married, then divorced. People put together weddings and horny hookups, but heaven ordains godly marriages. I always envisioned my wife and me carrying out our heavenly assignment together. Holy Matrimony is a sacred institution that should not be taken lightly, and there should not be any alternatives of a Plan B. Quitting is so prevalent, especially when times get rough. The tough times should go, but tough people tough marriages and tough people last. What makes Kingdom Marriage sweet is going through "for worse" in order to get to the "for better." Leaving takes absolutely no thought or effort. I do not want a cream puff that cannot take a storm. One of my all-time favorite people is Elder Victor Turner and he always told me that, "You want your wife to bless grits-and-eggs the same way that she blesses filet mignon." I never forgot that. There are a lot of shiny individuals, but not a large number who are great of character. In the hip-hop vernacular, "I want a ride-or die-chic". That simply means a person who is there through the good, the bad, and the ugly. A *Kingdom Marriage* is a covenant and not a contract. Contracts can be broken, as well as bought out. Blood, Sweat, and Tears are sown in covenant. Jesus is the Covenant keeper and if we keep Covenant with Him, we will keep Covenant with our mate. Do you have *A Kingdom Marriage* or a horny hookup?

"A PERFECT MATCH"

My first name is putty 'cause that's how you got me in your hands
My last name is genie, because your every wish is my command
I don't need a hot air balloon because with you I touch the sky
Why stay doped up on pain killers, it's your love that makes me high
This bed's all too big to be here by my lonesome
Without you lying next to me, I have no provision or purpose
It's like a play before the final act; someone comes and loses the curtains
I'm a nomad wandering aimlessly and my direction seems uncertain
There aren't enough numbers to count all of the ways, I want to grow old
     with you
It reminds me of the rent after the first of the month, our testimony to the
     world is past due
Talk about our marriage as being the epitome of one accord spiritually
We not only share the same Love, but not to mention the same kidney
God placed my rib in you but we have Siamese hearts that are attached
Think it not strange that no other family could answer the call, but my wife's a
     perfect match
This is a testimony to the multitudes, that JESUS still does signs and wonders
When the world gets involved, it ends in divorce, but with us, no man can put
     asunder
I looked in the dictionary, but there were no words to describe what you mean
     to me
So I guess I'll have to write my own book and call it The Book of Love
     Making History
Come judgment day, our memorial will not only be the gospel but will go down
     in history as a known fact
Come Judgment Day, our memorial will not only be the gospel, but will go
     down in history as a known fact
When we receive our new names in the Book of Life, it will not say Bryan and
     Ora Love but will
read…

A PERFECT MATCH!!!

This is one of my favorites because this is based on the truth. I was residing in Atlanta, Georgia and was invited to a soiree. I read one of my psalms at a housewarming. There I met a beautiful lady named Myrtle who admired my psalm. She was there with her daughter and grandson. She informed me about her good friends, Bryan and Ora Love. Mr. Love had kidney failure and after numerous attempts to locate a family donor, the search was to no avail. No one had the match except…his wife! Now I understand why Adam responded in the manner he did, after God woke him up and presented Eve unto him. Adam responded, "Bone of my bone and flesh of my flesh." This is a miracle! Therefore a man should leave his mother and father and shall cleave to his wife (Genesis 2:24). Not only do they share the spirit and soul tie, but the same kidney! Indeed, the kidney worked and because, how can two walk together unless they agree (Amos 3:3)? I get chills every time I think, talk, or write about. This is the epitome of *A Kingdom Marriage* at its finest! This is wonder for the world to see what can happen when the two are on one accord. I hope that this commentary will rescue someone's marriage that's in trouble. Keep the faith and finish your course. The difficult part is becoming one. It takes practice, effort, commitment, constancy, and consistency. Destiny awaits all marriages if Christ is the Chief Cornerstone of the relationship. All they have to do is look to each other and not away from each other. Husbands and wives, if you want, A Perfect Match, all you have to do is look inside each other to find what you are looking for. Remember, *A Perfect Match* is *A Kingdom Marriage* made in love for Bryan and Ora Love.

"GOD'S LEADING LADY" (PART 2)

I need you to come and rescue me from my island of loneliness
There was a vacancy in my heart, until you evicted love's homelessness
My house is not a home unless you grace it with your presence
The way my stomach butterflies when I see you, reminds me of my adolescence
Dear Ms. Beloved, you are the Alpha and Omega of my heart
Our union will end in destiny, but Holy Matrimony is where we start
If I had to label you a number, you are the perfect number seven
I'm in the Garden of Eden because my experience of being with you, have been
    nothing short of heaven
You have entered into the Holy of Holies into the city of my soul
Though we will go through winter in our relationship, my love for you will
    never wax cold
Come and take a trip on my peninsula of ecstasy
I refuse to rest until you're in a church aisle standing next to me
Out of all the peculiar daughters in Zion, you my dear, have set the bar
When I inquired the elders of your character, they proclaimed: "a virtuous
    woman is who you are"
I'm so delighted that I could fall in love with someone like you
I have never met a woman who reminds me of a marathon and I'm gonna run
    my love you
If I had to list what I like about you there are simply too many commas
Before I let anyone disrespect our covenant, it would be death before dishonor
You are my one true soul's desire, for GOD has anointed you to carry my
    babies
Heaven has hired you, promoted, and made you the CEO of my life as…

GOD'S LEADING LADY!!!

I did not intend to write a sequel, however, the leading lady was playing her role so well, and I had to pen her again. When you have a virtuous woman you have to send out Love Signals to her with hopes that she'll receive them from you. If you are a faithful man she will! Bobby Brown would say, "She's a special kind if girl that makes you feel good inside." *God's Leading Lady* plays her part because she is directed by God and led by the Holy Ghost, she embodies the fear of the Lord, compassion diligence, the law of kindness in her tongue, her husband trust and her children arise to call her blessed. More important she is willing to be led. Her words are gracious and seasoned with salt even when the man is wrong. She respects her covering and as Proverbs 14:1 states, "A wise woman builds her house, but a foolish woman tears it down with her own hands." *God's Leading Lady* ALWAYS is constructive and never destructive (except when she is tearing down strongholds); she is proactive and never reactive; she is diligent and does not eat the bread of idleness; and lastly she fears God (high regard, reverence) and hates the kingdom of darkness. Heaven favors *God's Leading Lady* or the daughters of Zion. She is willing to listen to wise counsel, keeps a clean house, and has a servant's heart. She is not flashy, does not flaunt what she has but what she carries is faith, possesses the anointing and the GLORY of God. God's Leading Lady is weighty, not because of her ring finger, but because she wears the Glory. The elders in the city know her husband because of who she is unto him...VIRTUOUS. God's Leading Lady is in Heaven's Hall-of- Fame in her husband's heart. He is her leading man. God's Leading man. *Who's That Lady?* The husband is her leading man. *God's Leading Lady*...coming to a life near you!

"WHEN TWO DESTINIES MEET"

Ev'rytime we make love, we intercede on each other's behalf
When you kiss me, I'm more of a man, but when you don't, I feel less than half
Before you showed up, love was my enemy, for as long as I can remember
Why celebrate February 14th, when you're my Valentine from January to
    December?
The time is near and won't be long, 'because I'll be comin' around the
    mountain when you call
If there's ever a time you shall stumble at love, I'll catch you before you fall
Both Satan and hell are trembling, when my wife and I get into bed
He never takes a vacation from tempting me, and lusts to give me a counterfeit
    instead
You tempt me when I'm fasting and I desperately want to devour you
I know what it's like to receive bread from heaven, for your love is my soul food
GOD has chosen, ordained, and anointed me to be your champion lover
At night, when it gets cold climb on top of me, and be my righteous cover
When I come home, you give me a hero's welcome, like I just got home from
    Iraq
You prayed for a dog in-the- bedroom, and your body's my Scooby Snack
Your body is my altar and when we become one, its awesome praise and worship
Because we're husband and wife, angels smile, because they know our
    matrimony is perfect
I'll run your bath water, give you a massage, wash, and anoint your feet
You'll see GOD's face ev'rytime we make love, and after I'm done, I'll rock you
    to sleep
Heaven smiles each time our legs intertwine and when our two hearts meet
The art of a husband-and-wife making love just isn't physical, but a ministry
    of . . .

WHEN TWO DESTINIES MEET!!!

The consummation between a husband-and-wife is spiritual, divine, and holy. It's a combination of two histories to equal one destiny. Consummation is a ministry in and of itself. There is nonverbal communication, healing, restoration, exhortation, and deliverance. Hell already trembles when marriages are on one accord, but also has a Maalox moment when they consummate, not only in their physical bedroom, but in the bedroom of their hearts. The bedroom is a sacred, behind-the-veil place. It is the *Softest Place on Earth*. Hearts become vulnerable, free, and all wounds are healed because the glory light of God cleanses ALL SOUL WOUNDS (Katie Souza)! The opposite of love is not hate, but fear. Perfect love casts (drives out fear) and fear hath torment (1 John 4:18). Spiritual warfare takes place when a husband-and-wife are intimate. No one feels embarrassed because of their vulnerability. This is the same weight of glory that covered both Adam and Eve before the fall of mankind. They were covered in so much glory, they were unaware of their nakedness. Glory covers the nakedness (flaws, disappointments, embarrassment, and insecurities, fears, etc.) that husband and wives individually embody. Love covers a multitude of sins and love making covers one another in sweat! Destinies are like two trains on opposite tracks coming from opposite directions, and meeting. The key is for two people to get on the same track and on the same train without derailing, crashing, and exploding. Both trains are carrying precious cargo and both must rely on the leading of the Holy Spirit to arrive at the designated place. The time has arrived for both parties to leave their "baggage" on their separate boxcars in order to ride on the "Midnight Train" to destiny. The parties that are engaged must board on *Love's Train*. It's time to unload everything that would add luggage to your relationship. There is a difference between adding luggage versus adding weight. The weight is glory is the presence of God. Stay tuned for *When Two Destiny's Meet*...coming soon to a train station and a marriage near you!

"WHAT GOOD IS"

What good is a bed, without you lying next to me?
What good is being a mother, if you didn't have kids from me?
What good is a laboratory without having chemistry?
What good is KINGDOM work, without us in ministry?
What good would my life be, if you weren't attached to me?
How nervous will hell be, when heaven joins you and me?
What good will our house be, if we didn't serve the LORD?
What good would our blueprints be if our architect ain't the LORD?
What good is your father, if he can't discern your husband is me?
What good is your father, if he didn't give you away to me?
What good is an altar, if I don't invite you to come?
What good are my family priorities, if my wife ain't number one?
What good is our wedding, if God doesn't bless our marriage?
What good would your hands be, if both ring fingers didn't have carats?
What good is faith, if you have to see it?
What good is GOD'S WORD, if you don't believe it?
What good is soul winning, without being an effective witness?
What good is workin' in the KINGDOM, if it ain't bout GOD's business?
What good are eagle eyes, if they don't allow me to see?
What good is a love seat, if you're not sitting next to me?
What good is a sweet tooth, if you're not my cavity?
And R. Kelly is a liar, because you're my Chocolate Factory?
What good would the devil be, if he wasn't the "World's Greatest Liar?"
What good would the church be, if it wasn't on fire?
What good is bein' in love, if you're not in it with me?
What good would your answer be, if it wasn't "YES" to me?
What good is a multiple choice, unless you fill-in- the-blank with me?
So what I'm really trying to say is . . .

WILL YOU MARRY ME?

W hat *Good Is?* Good is you lying next to me! Good is the two of us in the same room and making eye contact without saying a word, yet knowing exactly what our eyes mean. Good is holding you so tightly that all of the pain that you've ever experience comes out. Good is laying my hands on you praying for you. Good is leading you, then speaking into your life. Because I desire for you to reach your destiny in the Kingdom, it is my priestly duty to respond to my ability in God. Good is me being your love seat so you can rest on me. Good is me lying on your lap and you rubbing my head. Good is you not taking advantage of me, if I tell you my vision, then protecting it. Good is everything that you are to me! Remember, she will do him good all the days of her life! Good is the church coming back to its rightful place. The church will no longer be labeled a Rip Van Winkle church, but will transform to an insomniac church. She will be restless and work tirelessly for souls to be saved. Good is the Holy Ghost burning through all the impurities, spot, blemishes, and wrinkles out of our lives. Good is the two of us drinking lemonade in our rocking chairs, communicating about how we got over. Good is you calling me on my job to inform me that you're pregnant (after we get married)! Good is your father giving you away to me, and my grandmother giving me away to you. Good are all these things working together for our good. And everything God made was good, especially you and me. *What Good Is?* describes a love that can never be quenched.

"I NEED YOU TO SURVIVE"

A man doesn't have a complete day, unless he laughs, cries, and thinks
I laugh after I cry tears of joy, and when I think of you, I can't sleep a wink
In the dark, my pillow and I would taste my tears
Now my sheets are as dry as dead man's bones, and ever since you came, love
    lives here
But God broke the curse in my life, then attached you to me
My deliverance has finally come and today, my heartache ends
The LORD has scattered all my enemies and ordained you as my closest kin
I could have any love I want, but you and I are the perfect fit
You'll go down in the Lover's Hall-of- Fame, because you're the only woman,
    to whom I'll commit
Just to be with you, I'd climb the highest mountain, and swim the deepest sea
I'd pawn all my valuables and sell my possessions, that's how much you mean
    to me
Call me the book of Isaiah, because before you answered, I already called
I'll call you solar system, because my whole world revolves around you
The quarterback and you're my wide receiver, and I'm gonna throw all my love
    to you
I wanna take you to love school and you are my favorite subject
Refer to me as the Dom Perrignon of romance behind closed doors, and the
    perfect gentleman in public
When I was in intensive care, your arms were the life supports that keeps me alive
I guess it's safe to say, that you can call me Hezekiah Walker because . . .

I NEED YOU TO SURVIVE!!!

The greatest person God created for a man is a woman. A woman is the lifeline to a man. A good woman can make a man desire better for himself. A good woman can encourage instead of discourage, builds up instead of tears down, and respect him at all times. A good man is never ashamed to tell his woman, *I Need You To Survive*. A virtuous woman can please a man. The intensive care of her arms will keep him alive. Her virtue, prayer, respect, and love will be his life support. A woman can give a man life, then provide vitality to anything that is considered comatose or flat lined in his life. She is a queen and the mother of King Lemuel in Proverbs 30: 1-9 who gave sound advice to her son on how he is to rule as a king. She also is the one who advised her son what to look for in verses 10-31, which is a Proverbs 31 Woman. In a world where the man's voice is being silenced, the man is emasculated, effeminized, homosexualized, sodomized, and transgenderized, he needs a woman that can intercede, prophesy, and speak those things that be not as though they were into his eternal spirit. Bishop Hezekiah Walker penned the song which inspired the title to this piece of work. This type of woman won't harm you with words from her mouth. She speaks a word both in-and-out of season of exhortation and never degradation. She builds up her house with her own hands and looks well to the ways of her household. The well in the city of her soul never runs dry. The Wellspring of her life is so deep that her spiritual daughters can be refreshed, revived, and renewed. You need her to not only give you a drink, but your camels, and the servant's camels! Faithful men are in dire need of this kind of woman in their life to complete the assignment. I'm sending out Love *Signals* and am belting out these words unto her… *I NEED YOU TO SURVIVE*!!!

"A LEAGUE OF YOUR OWN"

The first time I saw your face, Cupid shot his arrow, then my heart was under attack

I'm the quarterback of your love, and when we go into overtime, I'll keep running back

My dentist told me to stay away from sweets, because you give me cavities

You pull me up when I falling down, that's why I call you my gravity

The doctor prescribed a dose of you to take care of my love sickness

You medicate my soul and I'll tell the world of Jehovah as my Witness

My dreams are now reality, since you are here by my side

Why die and go to heaven when forever's in your eyes?

Let me cover you like the morning dew and rain on you like a parade

My love is your refuge in the wintertime and in the summertime, my arms are your shade

When my life was an accident waiting to happen, you were the caution light to slow me down

By myself, my destiny was impossible to complete, but you've given new meanings to somehow

First, I'll be the man God called me to be while single, for I refuse to be a divorcee

Marriages fail because people are looking for what they want, instead of being who they're supposed to be

I'll call you puzzling because you possesses all the pieces that's well put together

I call you Ne-Yo, since you are Fabulous, 'cause baby girl you *Make Me Better*

It's hard to explain the effect you have on me, and I would just call it *Square Biz*

My heaven is right here with you and I never have to go home with a moan

When God created you a virtuous woman, he made you in . . .

A LEAGUE OF YOUR OWN!!!

I liken this psalm to the Professional Sports League of Women (PSLW) who are world-class athletes. The women that I had my eye on was the best woman in the league, which made her in a league of her own. She was one of the greatest woman that a man is privileged to have met. Every man meets at least one, maybe two ladies in his lifetime that he desires to change for. This lady that I had my eyes on was not only the league MVP (Most Valuable Player), but was the MVP of my life. She reminded me of the greatest selling album of all time. She was a *Thriller* to me, because I yearned for her to become the *Lady In My Life*. I was in calm emotional state when I wrote this psalm. No matter how erratic my emotions are, I am at my best when I write about who I envision for myself. Nothing or no one else matters and no one takes precedence when I put pen to paper. Writing about my wife takes me places that no one but heaven can take me. Heaven is her address. God just gave her a physical body in order for her to marry me and to carry out our assignment. God has drafted her in the *Lover's Hall-of-Fame* and then carefully placed her in *A League Of Her Own*.

"THE LOVE WE HAVE (STAYS ON MY MIND)"

Your breasts stand up tall like the green cedars in Lebanon
I was walking through life on the moon, but inside your arms, you turn on my
    alarm
Your teeth and eyes are pure white like goat's milk
And when I run my fingers through your hair, it feels like purple silk
As a round, young virgin, it is my priestly duty to protect your womanly virtue
Since your father allowed me to date you,
I'll bring you back seven minutes before curfew
You give me a hero's welcome ev'ryday as if I was a soldier in Iraq
I'm always in the Emergency Room, because when you touch me, my heart goes
    under attack
When you stare at me, your eyes are tender as two young does
Each time I look at your Coca Cola bottle silhouette, I want to come out of my
    clothes
Because your spirit is perfect, there are no flaws in you
I feel like the best man at the reception, so I'll propose a toast to you
Your lips are sweet as the Last Supper's wine
For I am intoxicated by your kiss, and when the cop stopped me, I was arrested
    for DUI
Indeed, you are the soul food that gives me sustenance and you're the main
    course that's on my plate
You can take a vacation on my love, anytime your will is to escape
I never consume alcohol, but if I did, you'd be my favorite drink
I'm an insomniac, because every time I think of you, I cannot sleep a wink
I searched the world over and I've come to the conclusion, that a lady like you
    is hard to find
There is no substitute when you're away from me because . . .

THE LOVE WE HAVE (STAYS ON MY MIND)!!!

The Dells originally recorded, *The Love We Had Stays On My Mind* in 1971, then later recorded by Dru Hill in 1998. I was in an old R&B mood when I wrote this psalm. I always loved old school music because there always was a message behind the music and a message in the messenger delivering the song. I joined Phi Beta Sigma Fraternity Incorporated and we had a singing group that consisted of myself, Anthony "Amp" Wilcox, Dr. Jake Golden IV, Jonathan "John" Roberts, and Tim Lee Wright, who was the genius and wrote all the plays for the African Americans Studies department. We used to have an event entitled, *A Night With The Sigma's* where Tim allowed everyone to showcase their talents. When I wrote this, I was thinking of a love that always stayed on my mind. The relationship in the song did not last, neither did mine last, which is the reason you are reading this now. I'm looking for a love (Bobby Womack) that I cannot shake or better yet, doesn't shake me! This young lady treats me so well because she is in *A League Of Her Own*. I go through obsessive and compulsive thoughts daily of this type of love. As a result, the love we have (present tense) stays on my mind. Have you ever had someone who is always in your thoughts? Love will make you do things that you said that you would never do. Let the church say . . . AMEN! She was beautiful, both inside and out. Beauty was her name, but her beauty was more than skin-deep. She makes me look at my life and aspire to do better. Her love is captivating, exhilarating, and reinvigorating. Her love is a breath of fresh air and like Toni Braxton, makes me Breathe Again. I'm thinking about you now darling. *THE LOVE WE HAVE (STAYS ON MY MIND)*, and it's coming to a heart near you!

"MORE THAN WORDS"

The closest I am to God is when I look into your eyes
Never again will I worry about a crackerjack kind-of- love, because baby, you
    are the prize
Let you and I get on this plane of love called romance
When I need to take a trip to ecstasy, I'll book you in advance
Heaven sent you to me when I yearned to experience virtue in its purest form
Our bodies will static cling like dryer sheets and if we keep this up, a love
    child will be born
I was homeless until I find permanent residence in your arms
God it wasn't landlord that evicted pain from your heart, because he knew
    that's where I belong
What can be a more natural that us being together?
When people see us, we remind them of Siamese twins, because we belong
    together
You're the drug that's got me hooked and I'm an all-out junkie
Loving you is my rehab and you're the best addiction a man could ever have
I need you like a blind man needs to see
"Fire and Desire" consumes me and the chariot that took Elijah up couldn't
    carry me
When my mind needs to be renewed, I close my eyes and think of you
Any anytime I crave a taste-of -honey, I bite into you because you're my sweet
    tooth
Ev'rytime we make love, I want to please you like there's no tomorrow
Each moment you touch me, I am debt-free, and I never have to borrow
I was a loser being away from you, and being without you is absolutely absurd
Though a dictionary can define every human emotion known to man,
There's none to describe you because you are to me . . .

MORE THAN WORDS!!!

I was in a state of speechlessness when I wrote this. I could not think of any words to write on my paper. Rarely do I ever get writer's block, but I also had a case of lover's block! I knew how special it would be to describe what my future wife means to me. There are no words in the English vernacular that could do her justice. Webster's Dictionary cannot define her as Jehovah as my witness. This woman is indeed *Heaven's Girl,* and everything that is a citizen of heaven, has its own language. I will dwell with my wife according to knowledge, as I study her to show myself approved unto God, a husband who needeth not to be ashamed, and rightly dividing a boy from a man. Our love will be an eternal love song before the canopy of heaven. Our relationship is "More Than Words." The only thing that can define our Holy Matrimony is *Book of Life.* When it opens on Judgement Day, the angels will sing an *Ode To Joy!* As the Alleluia Chorus sings the sheet music of our love, this will create a beautiful melody that will make Satan envious. As we stand before the throne on Judgment Day concerning our Holy Matrimony, Jesus will say, WELL DONE!!!

"I'M GONNA TO MAKE YOUR KINGDOM COME"

You'll make R. Kelly envious because of the *Love Signals* that you have sent me
But the kind of love that I'm talkin' 'bout is spiritual, the kind that opened my
    blind eyes to see
You've got that kind of love that made Jimi Hendrix smoke *Purple Haze*
And you are the *Southern Girl* that kept Frankie Beverly stuck inside a Maze
I'm a track star because I'm runnin' with you to Tyler Perry, J'Caryous
    Johnson, Shelly Garrett, and David E. Talbert plays
Now the Lord has established my goings, and you came the moment I changed
    my dogmatic ways
Never would I fathom that I could be monogamous with one person
My life was filled with doubt, however lovin' you is the only thing that's for
    certain
Every day is a new experience for me, each time that I am with you
GOD rested on the seventh day to make you because you were no work at all
Cinderella has nothin' on you, 'cause you were born to ball
When the news reported an armed robbery, it was your heart that I planned
    to steal
And my last request on death row would be your body as my favorite meal
In the bedroom, I'll go the distance, like a championship title bout
Each time I enter into your sacred gates, you'll remember how good GOD
    is and shout
When I need to get closer to heaven, I'll make love to you
And since GOD wants me to submit, I'll lie underneath you
GOD made you a perfect number seven so that you could be my number one
Be it so on earth as it is in heaven, because tonight . . .

I'M GONNA TO MAKE YOUR KINGDOM COME!!!

I was working at Mutual's Benevolence Society on Barnard Street in Savannah, Georgia as a bouncer in the club. I wrote this psalm on a napkin while DJ Darren B was killing it on the turntables. There are all different kinds of flavors of women in a club. The music was blasting and the atmosphere was electric. In spite of the distractions, I could still hear the voice of God. Although none of the women were worthy of saying, "I Do," there always were a few who caught my attention. If I didn't think soberly, I knew that I would end at intersection of Desire Street and Passion Boulevard. Only nine days away from my 31st birthday, I could feel my spirit changing. I yearned for something meaningful and lasting. However, my heart still had keloid scars on it. I was fearful of becoming vulnerable, especially with this population of ladies. In the club atmosphere, people are only looking to have a good time. The theme is don't love me, just love what we do! I was writing with the mindset of not only taking your body where it has never gone before, but also taking your soul there as well! I could have my physical needs there, but nothing spiritual. This featured psalm was given in a secular environment. Indeed, God does have a sense of humor. I'm going to bring the Kingdom to fruition inside of you. I'm going to love you so deeply, that everything that was unlocked will open! Heaven is using me to fulfill my relationship assignment with you. When we consummate, our love will explode like the fireworks on 4th of July. Every day will be Juneteenth Day in our bedroom. I will make love to you like I am free. I will only be a slave to your love. The Kingdom has come to our bedroom because my kingdom will come to a bedroom inside of you!

"HOW SOON"

I must have arrhythmia because ev'rytime I'm around you, my heart skips a beat
You are as down home as grandma's homemade recipe, for you are truly a
    Georgia Peach
Because of you, I'd register and if you run for election, you've got my vote
I wanna wrap my love around you like the skirt around your legs, I just wanna
    be close
I yearn for our spirits to be attached like Siamese twins
If anyone should ask your priority to me, I'll them, "the place where love begins
    and ends"
When your father inquires how close we are, I tell him you're my closest kin
Since my haters are questioning how I ended up with you, I'll simply respond
    by saying, "I love to win"
I'd hold my breath just so you can have fresh air to breathe
In order for our relationship to work, I'm leaving my parents' house so you and
    I can cleave
If you're in need of a breakthrough, I'll spend all night on my knees
I'll sow into you to reap my harvest, because darlin' you are the seed
Since I am love's prisoner, I don't wanna be bailed out
If I want my home to be complete, I need you to be the fragrance of this house
You are my eternal delight and I beseech you to rest inside my shade
Though a brand new garment will wax old, my desire for you will never fade
I long to graze between your breasts like a cow inside his pasture
I never wanted you for what's between your legs because it is your heart that
    I'm after
In the city of my soul, I knew you were to incubate my vision in your womb
GOD had early spoken our union would come to pass, but hell is trembling
    and asking . . .

HOW SOON?

The R&B singer, Joe, penned a song called *How Soon* back in 1997 when I was at Valdosta State University. The song was about him being in a long-distance relationship with a young lady who was a professional and her job promoted her to a position out-of-town. How many of you have ever been in a long distance love affair? You are caught between a rock-and-a hard place, not to mention sinking in quicksand with cement shoes. Am I selfish for wanting them here with me or do I love them enough to let them go to pursue their career? I never want them to blame me for why their dream did not come to pass. I could not live with that guilt and condemnation. Sacrifice is the key. Get here by carpet, airplane, train, automobile, or by Pony Express! I don't care how you get here, get here if you can (Oleta Adams). I was in a long-distance relationship and the conversations were getting serious. The time had come for us to see one another. She was in Jacksonville as I drove to surprise her. When I called her, she was surprised, happy, and confused. She was an event that her friend held and did not want to be inconsiderate. I understood and needless to say, I drove back to Savannah in the rain. We still communicated via phone. When I talked about meeting her, there was always something that got in the way. I saw pictures via internet and phone. I was in for a *Trapped In The Closet* experience. Let's just say that this person was not who she said that she was. Readers, do your due diligence and investigate before you invest. This person was a fraud and had several guys thinking the same way. She was scandalous. You have already done the math to see that our relationship equation equaled zero. I know that you want to know did we see each other. The answer is **NEVERUARY!!!**

"YOU ARE THE PRIZE"

When a woman is joined to her Boaz, she will also possess his vision
When a man finds his rib, he inherits her submission
Each night when I cover you in prayer, I lift you up like a blood-stained banner
For the times that I was hungry in the city of my soul, GOD sent you as my
    manna
Our honeymoon night will be the consummation that heaven shall never forget
Death is too weak to separate us, and the only thing that'll come between us is
    sweat
Granted I've failed at many endeavors, however the two things I'm most proud
    of in my life
And that is accepting JESUS as my LORD and Personal Savior and finding
    you as my wife
When I wanted GOD to grant me favor, heaven sent you to me
When I needed to clean the house, you were the broom to sweep me off my feet
I have come to remove the splinters from your soul and replace it with joy and
    laughter
If your heart was my finish line, then it is first place that I'm after
We are a divine combination, and we got together like peas-and-carrots
When the Holy Spirit joined us in Holy Matrimony, HE created a kingdom
    marriage
Because I committed my works unto the Lord, my thoughts are now established
And ev'ry time you touch me, the in-laws buy a new baby carriage
From the first time our spirits bared witness, I knew my life was just beginning
Destiny sent an assignment for me to experience an angel in disguise
Never will I ever have to buy Cracker Jacks again because baby…

YOU ARE THE PRIZE!!!

Cracker Jacks inspired me to pen this. When I was knee-high to a duck, I would buy Cracker Jacks solely for the prize inside. Just as sure as they don't put good prizes in the Cracker Jack box anymore, it's even more difficult to find a prize the pride in a ring box anymore! God has put her in a box to be preserved her for the man. *Heaven's Girl* always is the prize for a faithful man servant. Cracker Jacks are sweet but not compared to her natural sugar. She is the natural sweetener to my life. Strange women are full of artificial sweeteners, dyes, lies, and preservatives. She is the prize that men should marry, and she will give you what she prizes…her heart. Guys, if you have her heart, you have everything else, take care of her heart, and her heart will take care of you. I was envisioning her body as my last meal on death row. She is my sweet tooth. The dentist has to pull all of my teeth because they are rotten. A man is appointed once to die, but after that is the Judgment, but how many can say that they were sweet-toothed to death! My wife will be the prize of my purpose, the prized possession of my soul, and the prophecy of my prayer. She is the object of my desire, and because I delight myself in the Lord, she is the desire of my heart. This lady is the handkerchief that wipes away my tears, and I am her courage to face her fears. She is the lady that King Lemuel's mother told him that he should look for as a Proverbs 31 Woman. This misty lady is indeed my *Voyage to Atlantis*. My rib is the psalm I write about, the song I belt out, and the thought that I think about. I never have to worry about Cracker Jacks again or what's inside the box because baby, *You Are The Prize*!!!

"WE"RE TOGETHER"

When I asked GOD to deliver me to my destiny, I was sent to find you
When I asked the Holy Spirit what is heaven like, HE showed me a vision
of you
For all those sleepless nights that I desire refuge, I will run inside your arms
When the city of my soul longs to be awakened, you turn on my alarm
The angels suffer from severe depression, since you were sent to me on
assignment
I'd do a lifetime bid as love's prisoner, but only if you're with me in solitary
confinement
I'll never experience fulfillment in this lifetime if I'm not connected to you
We were already married from the moment I saw you, I knew I was meant
for you
Just the thought of us being together is as natural to me as breathing
Your touch causes me to whistle like a tea kettle, you always keep me steaming
I am willing to experience everything that Holy Matrimony has to offer
Since our Heavenly Father has given me the right away, I'll meet you at the
altar
When it seems we can never come to terms on an issue and our hearts are in
need of patience
GOD has drawn us nigh to each other through the spirit of reconciliation
There is nothing more rewarding than fulfilling heaven's purpose in this life
And the greatest compliment a man could ever receive is to have a virtuous
woman as his wife
I was stuck in quicksand with cement shoes, until your love placed me on a
solid foundation
Although I've received numerous applause for my carnal accolades, nothing
compares to your standing ovation
Yes, divorce is on the rise in the church, and couples divorce after a forecast of
stormy weather
Only because our souls have been anchored in JESUS is the sole reason why

WE'RE TOGETHER!!!

The greatest sentence in a love language is "You and I are meant to be". To abbreviate it for the sake of time is *We're Together*. My aunt Veronica, who lives in the state of Texas, called to inform me that her church, Abundant Life Cathedral, was hosting a marriage retreat. The theme for this 2009 event was entitled, *We're Together*. She asked if I could simply write something for the extravaganza. Despite never being asked to write for a church function before, I did not want to let her, myself, and more importantly God down. I simply prayed for the words to be downloaded in my spirit, so I knew that there would not be any pressure on me to get the job done. Heaven was endorsing me, and the Holy Ghost was leading me. I began to think about a *Dream Girl* and how important she would be in my life. When everyone asked me about our relationship status, I would confidently say, *We're Together*. Not only are we together physically in a relationship, but more importantly, we are knit together spiritually. How can two walk together unless they agree (Amos 3:3)? The in-laws cannot divide us, the husband's mother cannot drive a wedge between us, the wife's father cannot spoil the daughter with money, and the devil cannot steal our joy. Why? The answer is, *We're Together*. If nothing shall be able to separate us from the love of God, then nothing shall be able to separate us from us loving each other! *We're Together*...coming to households and in stores everywhere.

"HELPLESSLY IN LOVE"

Many women have been called, but God has chosen you to become a part of my life

Many have the potential of a princess, but you're the royal queen that is anointed to be my wife When I was trapped in the Lost and Found, your love was the only thing strong enough to claim me

Heartbreak tied me in bondage before you unlocked the door to my heart and now I'm free

Your skin is as smooth as Egyptian silk, and you've earned the title Ms. Savoir Fair

You stick close to me like a shadow, 'cause when I look over my shoulder, you are there

Each time you pray, I desire to be your hands when you give thanks

And when my house is out-of-order, you're the commanding officer to keep rank

God caused me to fall into a deep sleep, and He created you from my rib

You're my help meet to manifest my destiny and encourage my heart so I can live

God has charged me not to be a lid, but my wife's cover

My assignment is to be fruitful, multiply, replenish, subdue, and have dominion, but to also be your champion lover

The day that I met you is when I felt my life begin

I was a backslider until I married an angel, now I no longer sin

I would rather go blind than to see you with another

Winter, Spring, Summer, Fall, from January to December, I'm your death do us part cover

I get so emotional when I'm inside your arms, since I've been away from home for so long

My heart is the blank sheet music so that you can create melody to our love song

I'm found guilty on all counts in Lover's Court, and my hands do fit the glove

When the judge asked how do I plea, I throw myself at the mercy of the court

All because I'm...

HELPLESSLY IN LOVE!!!

I was listening to the R& B group, New Edition's Greatest Hits when I ran across this hidden gem of a song. This phone slipped through my musical rolodex since I pride myself on various genres of music. If you listen to the lead singer, Ralph Tresvant on his track, he reminded me of the doo-wop and Motown groups from yesteryear. Can you hear the Temptations' David Ruffin belting out from every note from his soul? This young lady was indeed my temptation, for she provoked me unto good works. She provoked me to be a better man, to never settle for mediocrity, and pushed me to my destiny. I was not in a relationship, however, I was writing prophetically about who I desired. How can you help being helplessly in love with a young lady like this? She was my new addition and yes, she can stand the rain! Romeo and Juliet were in love like this. Donnell Jones sang to this lady about being scared to experience a *Love Like This*. And you who are reading are yearning to be *"Helplessly In Love"* like this. This song happens to be one of my favorite songs from New Edition. It is a timeless classic just like the old groups of yesteryear. If you are ready to be Helplessly In Love, get ready for the new addition and the *New Edition* of your life.

"PRIZED POSSESSION"

You are an African Violet that springs through the fallow ground of these
    wordly streets
You are a lily among thorns in this wayward world, for your virtue is so unique
To me, you are indescribable and worth more than the cost of a wedding in June
You are the bud on an almond tree, and no matter what the season, you are
    always in bloom
You remind me of a crisp fall evening in October at the Coastal Empire Fair
You are the delicate flower that Minnie Riperton pins in her lovely hair
You are the peace that leads me besides the quiet stream
My life was an eternal sleep walk, but when I woke up, you became my dream
I find solace when I rest inside the shade called your loving arms
I'm your boa constrictor since I yearn to wrap you up in my charms
Daughters in Zion, do not arouse or awaken love until God so desires
Allow love to develop into a commitment instead of lust an unquenchable fire
Guard your heart with due diligence, and let your femininity to become a
    locked garden
May your husband of your youth pick your flower so that God doesn't have to
    beg your pardon
Liken your anointing to a vault whose defense is impregnable
Never allow immorality's door to be open to a reputation that's detestable
I have gone to prepare a place for you, and that, my dear, is my heart
You can send love an invitation of welcome and if you open the door,
    it will never part
Before God and the church, I am ready to decree a public confession
And when the world desires to know your value to me, I'll proclaim that
    you're my

PRIZED POSSESSION!!!

A A Proverbs 31 Woman is a *Prized Possession* because she is a rare find and a priceless jewel. I was dealing with a barrage of emotions during this psalm because my mother was in Grady Hospital in Atlanta, Georgia. I did not know if she was going to recover from her aneurysm. Dr. Sanjay Gupta was the Head Surgeon who operated on her, but Jesus was the Great Physician, not only in the operating room, but her life. I vividly remember writing this poem on the porch after TV One did a documentary on the great Minnie Riperton. She was a *Prized Possession* to the music industry and similiar to my wife's place in my life. A husband will protect his wife's virtue, honor, and reputation. More importantly, she values it because she knows her value. She knows her worth. She cannot be bribed or coerced, because Jesus purchased her redemption with his blood. *Prized Possession* is what Ronald "Mr. Biggs" Isley sang about in this song, which is where the title to the song came from. I wrote this psalm not knowing that my mother would pass eleven days later. I did not know that I would be performing a tribute. Being a *Prized Possession* means that you appreciate what the Lord has given you. She never manipulates her relationship because she holds them in high esteem. Remember, her goal is to do to him good all the days of her life! Trickery, deception, manipulation, and control are foreign to her. *Prized Possession* is one who builds up her home, and never tears them down with her own hands.

"LOVE NO LIMIT"

When I first laid eyes on you, I felt my life was just beginning
For God to send a virtuous woman such as yourself, I knew that I would have
    to stop sinning
What is this unfamiliar sound of opportunity rapping on my chamber door?
It's the knock of your love penetrating the dent in my heart, for this is
    something I can't ignore
Many times I've received an invitation to love's ball, I just could not afford to
    pay the fee
I'm doing a lifetime bid as your love slave, and the truth is I don't wanna be free
It's never far to Forever Land, if that's the destination you desire to travel
    with me
If you like what's inside my heart, please take all that you want from me
My nights are colder and much longer whenever you aren't near
Everyday feels like Halloween, ain't nothing but tricks live here
I know the grass is greener on the other side because the other side is you
I no longer play on artificial turf because I'll score a touchdown by
    marrying you
I was walking in quicksand in cement shoes until the day you found me
I sow tears on my pillow, hoping my harvest would reap you in my bed
I knew God favored me with royalty because you're the crown that sits upon
    my head
For years, I searched to discover you, the Lord's finest
You are the queen on the throne of my life, and I refer to you as your highness
Heaven has unclogged my ears in the Spirit and with your angelic voice, I
    hear it
I will take you where no man has ever gone before and you call it...

LOVE NO LIMIT!!!

There are no boundaries or limits to our love. It is so special when a man will go to love unlimited for his lady. No distance is too far, no mountain is too high, no valley is too low, no river is too deep, and there is no misunderstanding too complicated to separate the love between a man and a woman. I am in the presence of God when I am writing because I feel close to God. I will feel closer to God when my rib is presented to me. I was in a state of contentment when I wrote this psalm. I know that my wife would be my *Harvest For The World* as a result of all of the tears that I have sowed on my pillow. Because of her love, there will be no cap on our intimacy. There will never be a speed limit to our love because we are on cruise control. Our love will never get a ticket for reckless love because the Love Police has giving me the driving manual on the correct way to lose my love to satisfy my wife. If I ever need lights or fail to study to show myself approved unto God with this manual, the Holy Bible, the Holy Spirit will arrest me for reckless abandonment. With the exception of confessing to the crime (1 John 1:9). I do have the right to remain silent. I am given the charge of studying to be quiet. Husbands, your love should never have any limit if you love your wife as Christ loved the church and gave his life for it. Jesus gave Himself for his bride (the church), so husbands are to do the same for their wives. They are only called to give their lives for their wives and not their children. The husband is to leave his mother and father and cleave to his wife (woman-natural born Genesis 2:24). Children come into their parent's lives and not the other way around. Children should never interfere with the sacred institution of marriage. Wives are supposed to place their husbands first and not their children. Mothers who place their sons before their husbands are committing spiritual incest. Husbands and wives are in covenant. Parents and children have a contract. A child can become emancipated from their parents, but divorce was not so from the beginning. Mothers are treating their sons like the husband and treating their husbands like the son. Because the relationship is perverted between the mother and the son, the house is divided, which means it will not stand. How can two walk together unless they agree (Amos 3:3)? The wives and sons are in agreement, but the wives and husbands are divided because of the son. The son is leading the wife and the wife does not want to follow the husband. This is as the result of the husband wanting to discipline the son for immaturity and his folly. The mother is to nurture and love, and the father is to control and patrol. When the rightful order is established, there will be *Love No Limit* between a husband and wife. Husbands and wives should never allow the children to break up what God has joined.

"YOUR FINGER HAS FOUND MY RING"

Oh yes, I'm guilty of love in the first degree
And I sentence you to a lifetime of ecstasy between you and me
You're my bright-and-morning star, and when we consummate our love, you'll
    shine in your full glory
The virgin birth was already taken, but together you and I, are the second
    greatest story
If truth could speak, it would surely testify of your virtue
I was magnetically attracted, for that was what drew me unto you
When I found you, God showed me my purpose driven life
I was made debt free the moment you said "I DO" to become my wife
Finally, I've discovered a love song that's worth singing
In our bedroom, you're my dryer sheet because our bodies will be static clinging
Ev'ry time I dream of a runway, I envision you as America's Top Model
When I'm thirsty, my favorite drink is Coca-Cola since you are shaped like the
    bottle
We're the beautiful music that Donnie Hathaway and Roberta Flack created in
    the studio
I vow to water your *Secret Garden* so that the flower of your love will always
    grow
You give me fever, and you're the reason why I frequent a thermometer
Ev'ry time we touch, you awaken my desire, to keep me hot and bothered
There's a flash flood warning in my heart, your love has consumed me
I have waited with the patience of Job for my change to come, Hallelujah, my
    God has proved me
Now that heaven has joined us, I now have the faith to soar like a dove on
    eagle's wings
The scripture is fulfilled today because I found my good thing, but more
    importantly.....................

YOUR FINGER HAS FOUND MY RING!!!

It is the gospel truth that a man who finds a wife, findeth a good thing. Equally important is her finger finding my ring! When I was growing up, we had a saying that, "Finders keepers, loser's weepers!" God has hid her finger for only me. Yes, "I Do" like it, and I'm going to put a ring on it. She is my upgrade. My mama used to say, "If a man buys a large ring only means that he can afford more payments"! The size of the ring does not indicate the degree of a man's love for a woman. Ladies, stop being so shallow and playing yourself cheap. You have only planned for a wedding when you should have planned for a marriage! You are a strange woman. If you run into a woman like her, you better be like be like Usain, and Bolt in the opposite direction! A virtuous woman is the crown that sits upon his head (Proverbs 12:4). She not rest on my head, but she lives in my heart. Like Michael Jackson, she is a *"Thriller"* and I *Wanna Be Startin' Somethin* with her in our bedroom. Savannah was hosting a gospel talent showcase and I answered the call. I did not want to be like the rest of the contestants, so I decided to recite this psalm to the judges. I ended up advancing to the next round held at Savannah State University. Though I did not place, I opened some eyes. I was glad to be in the number one more time. My wife is the dryer sheet since our bodies will be static clinging! I already have a box, though my love no limit can never be boxed in! Would you like to see what's inside the box? You don't have to work for what already belongs to you. Because God has promised to do a complete work in us, we must position ourselves for the complete work to be done! After you have suffered a while, God will perfect, establish, strengthen, and settle you for such a time as this. You are my royalty and the queen of my heart. My mother in glory has passed the baton to you in the spirit as my wife because..

YOUR FINGER HAS FOUND MY RING!!!

"LOVE STREET"

Oh my darling, behind your veil are two young and tender doe eyes
I can safely say that the name on your birth certificate is Cracker Jack because
baby you are my prize
Indeed, you are the last woman I'll ever love, and I am your first
Your love reminds me of a Sprite and I'm going to obey my thirst, and drink
from the fountain of your love, it's time to obey my thirst
I desire to graze between your two breasts, like a cow in his pasture
Then our two heartbeats shall become one, for a soul tie is what I'm after
Please tell me what cloud did you come down on at this juxtapose of my life
I petitioned heaven for my latter rain, and God showered down on me the
perfect wife
You, my bride, are as refreshing to me as a Colorado mountain spring
Never again will you play hide and seek from me because your finger has
found my ring
My doctor says that I wasn't fit to be alone, and hope deferred is causing my
heart sickness
He prescribed to consistently knock on your chamber door just like a
Jehovah's Witness
We didn't cross each other by happenstance, this isn't just a case of boy meets
girl
I saw you in my dreams with a sickle in your hand, and the Spirit said you're
the harvest to my world
Surely goodness and mercy is following me, and that's why God sent me you
When you are created a Proverbs 31 woman, there is no flaw in you
Come quickly, My Beloved, our trip to the altar is long overdue
I honor you for keeping a locked garden, and like a soldier, I salute you
Now the fullness of time has come in our bedroom for both of our destinies to
meet
I will move my legacy inside your Blessed Boulevard and then we'll create a....

LOVE STREET!!!

I was in stepper's mood, and R. Kelly's *Happy People* CD influenced the title. What if the whole world lived on Love Street? Men's hearts will not fail them because of iniquity, and the love of many will never wax cold. There will be no more White Supremacy, racism, unjust laws, wars, and the root of it all, a desperately wicked heart. Every sin is the result of the condition of the heart. Truly, *Love's In Need Of Love* today. This is the street that I'm moving to because of my wife. We will no longer reside on Heartbreak Boulevard because that is a one-way, dead-end street. I want to get engaged, married, train up godly children, and do the Lord's will on this street. I cannot do anything without love (1 Corinthians 13). All recipes are a masterpiece with this main ingredient. One of the greatest blues singer, B. B. King said it best, The Thrill Is Gone. Love is not based on feelings because agape love means loving what's not lovable. People need love the most when they deserve it the least. God sent his son Jesus to die when we were at our worst, and were reconciled back to Him with unconditional love. My darling, love is who you are to me, and we will give love lessons to the birds and the bees! The title of our masterpiece is the *The Book of Love Making History* (the title of one of my poems). Can you tell me how to get, how to get to Love Street? We need directions to that street called love. Where is it? Jesus is the Way, the Truth, and the Life. You can only move there when the Holy Spirit is your compass. Love Street....moving to your heart and a community near you.

"YOU . . . MY WIFE"

For once in my life, next to Jesus, I've made my greatest decision by choosing you
I've decided not to walk away from my breakthrough by drawing closer to you
My arms are your loveseat, so lay back in my tenderness
All my life I've starved myself of companionship until you filled my emptiness
I realize that unconditional love is to love what's not lovable
That's the reason I'll stay during the winter of our relationship and persevere
   when it's not comfortable
You are indeed a helpmeet which means you are a proper, suitable fit for me
Our union has to be earned and purchased by a covenant, and in that dwells
   the spirit of unity
Relationships are designed to help you develop away from self
The enemy knows that when God joins a man and a woman, it's bad for his
   health
You are the beautiful melody in the morning that the mockingbird choir sings
I'll purposely allow you to play hide-and-seek by allowing your finger to find
   my ring
When I arose, the Holy Spirit revealed that our heavenly marriage is not an
   old wives' fable
Before I partake of a full course meal such as yourself, I must learn how to set
   your table
God has sent me on assignment to lift you up like a blood-stained banner
I'm gonna climb on top of you like my grandma's sofa in her living room, like
   a child wit' no manners
When we are rooted and grounded in love, we're directly connected to the
   ultimate power source
Because God is the Alpha and Omega of our faith, our most hated word is
   divorce
You are the greatest *Song In The Key Of Life*
Heaven has just begged my pardon, and declared me *Guilty*, then sentenced me
   to serve a lifetime bid in the person of....................................

YOU . . . MY WIFE!!!

My wife is who you are to me. You are personal to me, and you wear the title of the undisputed champion who won my heart. Inside you of is where I live, move, and will create another human being. You are my melody at midnight and the lyrics to my love song. You, my wife, are the songs in the key of my life. You are God's best helper that he could ever fashion for me. You are my forever Valentine 366 (LEAP YEAR) days a year because you make my heart leap this year. I gladly give you a standing ovation like the Dells. Though I received several accolades, I long for your applause. Heaven approves and endorses you for my life, and the Holy Ghost approves this message. You are one of the *Seven Wonders of The World*. To describe you, I would have to speak in my heavenly language. Because you are supernatural, I have the best of both worlds. You are an angel from heaven that is in the form of a natural woman. You are a representation and the epitome of a holy woman. You are Cleopatra, Nefertiti, and Sheba Baby. You are my Pam Grier and Kenya Moore to me. You are my *Harvest For The World*. When the world interviews me and ask who you are to me, I'll confidently respond.........................

YOU......MY WIFE!!!

"NUMBER ONE HIT"

Your love is like a full buffet that I never have to come back for seconds
Our relationship is at the top of heaven's charts, we're way past platinum
Your life is the perfect atmosphere for me to reach my destiny
I won't stop pursuing you until you're standing before the preacher next to me
We're the beautiful melody the angels sing in heaven
God's will be done concerning me when I position myself to find you in 2011
When destiny joins us, God will give us a standing ovation
And since our only debt is to love one another, the economy will ask us for a
     donation
Ev'ry time we make love our bodies sing in the perfect key
Your angelic voice sounds like all the instruments, and I changed your name
     to symphony
My arms are a custom made fit for you to dwell in
And your ocean-front property was the perfect temperature for my legacy to
     swim in
When I download my love to you, I'm gonna set your soul free
Then we'll teach the lifestyle of the birds and the bees to the birds and the bees
You are my life sentence of ecstasy, and I refuse to post bail
You're my Sunday morning church gossip that I can't wait to tell
God showed off when He designed you just for me
There's no way I could afford your virtue, so Jesus' blood purchased you for me
I get ants in my pants, to the point that I have a conniption fit
No doubt your love is a song worth singing, and that makes you my

NUMBER ONE HIT!!!

Since you are the greatest love song in the key of my life, it's safe to say that you are my Number One Hit. You are on the top of the charts of my heart. I have asked my mom to step aside leave and now she is the first runner up. You are platinum, and she is gold. My mother totally understands, and as a result, has placed the crown on your head. You are the queen that I refer to as your highness. You are the greatest song of all time that is a timeless classic. You are a masterpiece in *A League Of Your Own* and a designer's original. You are the blueprint that I want Christ to build my life with. Christ is the Chief Cornerstone that we will build our house upon. All other ground is sinking sand. *Number One Hit* is my favorite song thus far because you are the same lady the artist was referred to in the song. We blew up like Betty Jean and Lingeela, like the Zetas and Sigma's. You're a *Smooth Operator* like Sade, and we annihilate all competition like Amp and LJ. Why? It's all elementary my dear. You are the *Number One Hit*. You've got spiritual tenacity and intestinal fortitude. You are connected, committed, constant, and consistent to the things for the Kingdom of God. When the Book of Life opens, it will read, "Well done thou good and faithful servants" because your marriage was a *Number One Hit*! I'm sending out love signals to your spirit. Just give me the green light and I'll drive to your heart. When your finger finds my ring, the light will change from red to green. Together, we will create number one hits in the form of children.

"THE WORLD"S NATIONAL ANTHEM"

When I transition, I desire to share a one-room studio apartment with you in glory

And when the Lamb opens the Book of Life, our marriage will read *The Second Greatest Story*

The foundation of heaven will read Peter, Paul, James, and John

But as you receive your rewards from the Lord, your name will be on the jasper wall

If I never make another dime in this lifetime, all I need is the favor of God and your virtue

Since I can never fathom leaving you, I apologized to your father, because I'm bringing you back way past curfew

If your life were a song, hands down, you are a *Number One Hit*

When God spoke over our lives He called us his puzzle piece all because we're the perfect fit

If you were a drink, you would be the classic wine, Moet

Since we are the Ashford and Simpson of the Kingdom, we are a smashing duet

The vibration from your walk is so melodic that even the angels quiet their singing

We'll stick to each other like dryer sheets since our bodies will be static clinging

When the wind blows against your body, every instrument is heard

You provoke the heavens to go silent, and your music mutes the birds

Your angelic voice is the perfect pitch for my destiny, and you are the reason for my rhyme

There is no many ways to count your virtue that no clock will ever tell the time

From the moment I first laid eyes on you, my mind forgot ev'ry bad memory

That is why the doctor prescribed me to take a dose of you since you are my remedy

Our marriage is the picture that Adam and Eve envy to capture

God will use our ministry for heaven's glory, and our love song will be entitled.

THE WORLD'S NATIONAL ANTHEM!!!

Our marriage will be what Thomas Dorsey means to Gospel music in the Black church, what Motown meant to the sound of young America, what soprano means to my grandmother, what alto meant to Lucille Edwards, what *How I got Over* meant to Mahalia Jackson, what the Homestead means to the west side of Garden City, Georgia. I wrote this on my grandmother, Mother Louise Baxter's birthday. Our harmonious marriage will become the *World's National Anthem* to all heterosexual marriages. We will become a blueprint of how to treat each other as we dwell together according to knowledge. Indeed, we are *Solid* as a rock like Ashford and Simpson. Our relationship is Solid because our Holy Matrimony is built on the Rock of Jesus Christ of Nazareth. Heaven chose you to partner with me to be a suitable proper fit (help meet). The angels wrote the music to our relationship. After all, we are a smashing duet and a *Number One Hit*. Before the start of every event, as we pledge allegiance to our Lord and Savior, they will sing our love song, *The World's National Anthem*. Stay tuned, *The World's National Anthem* is coming to an eardrum near you.

"BEHIND YOUR VEIL"

The angels will propose a toast as they partake in the Holy Communion of our
    love
This union was ordained by the Father of lights coming down from above
Your body is my braille, and I'm gonna use my fingers to read you
My hands are like an octopus, and every night, I'm gonna feel you
Heaven is my reward if God raptures me, or if He allows me to stay here,
    either way I win
Our ministry is heaven's love song, because we'll rescue the world using our
    paper and pen
First, we'll start by holding divorce hostage, then bind it up forever
We will loose love in ev'ry relationship, and command marriages to stay
    together
I'll always fail the sobriety test since I'm intoxicated by your kiss
You're my genie in a bottle because your virtue grants my every wish
I'm one up on R. Kelly, you are my "Love Letter" that I'll read every day
Cupid evicted himself since you're my sweet Valentine that will permanently
    stay
We'll make love in two-part harmony, I'm the tenor that makes your soprano
    hit a high note
As soon as I experience touch withdrawals, your body's my perfect antidote
If you were on the radio, I could only stand to listen to your melody for only
    one hour
Your golden voice is the Quiet Storm and your station is called WLP, Love
    Power
I'm so elated that you're my television because I watch ev'ry episode
God gave me your heart combination, and I'm the only one, He'll allow to
    decode
When we consummate our love, your father will show the elders your trail
For I'm the priest who'll enter into your Holy-of-Holies when I go.......

BEHIND YOUR VEIL!!!

Behind your veil is the *Holy of Holies* where the presence of God is. The eternal glory or the weight of God resonates here. We now have access behind there because Jesus is the propitiation (atonement) of mankind's sin. This writing was special because this was my grandmother's seventy-third birthday. I was in the presence of God when I wrote this because I was shaking when I wrote this. This was one of two psalms that I wrote on this particular day. I was basking in the Shekinah glory of the Lord. Just like what Thomas Dorsey meant to Gospel music in the Black church, what Union Sunday School means to Clifton and Fairlawn, what the Homestead means to the Westside of Garden City, what *How I Got Over* meant to Mahalia Jackson, and what Louise and Lucille meant to each other, the same applies to our sacred love. A behind your veil relationship has to be earned. Intimate details are shared along with time and space. Hearts are exposed and motives are revealed. An exchange is made because strengths are exchanged for weaknesses. Making love to your wife is holy and consecrated. I will decode her body in any language. If I was blind, I would allow my fingers to run across her beautiful design as if it were braille. Going behind your veil is the softest place on earth. It is delicate, priceless, and no camera could capture this picture. She is a work of art, for she is fearfully and wonderfully made. This angel has no flaws in her spirit. There are no misunderstandings, wrath, bitterness, clamor, or divorce behind the veil. Love is pure, innocent, and holy. Husbands, behind the veil of her heart is where you belong. Miss Beloved, I am making my reservations to go where no man has ever gone before…. *Behind Your Veil*.

"TABLE OF CONTENTS"

You and I together are a brand, a standard of all relationships
If you were my woman, I would call you Gladys Knight, since you give me the
    "Pips"
You are the "Quiet Storm" that spins in heavy rotation all night long
I look forward to you changing your address inside these arms, and this is the
    place where you belong
We are a perfect blend of destiny and purpose, for we go together like
    peas-and-carrots
People describe us as the Marvin Gaye and Tammi Terrell of ministry,
    because our chemistry creates a harmonious marriage
You are the song of my life, and your voice is a timeless classic that I'd never
    turn off
As I'm stuck in the maze called life, you lead me to green pastures when I'm
    lost
Your heart is the foundation for me to build my dreams upon
I was walking through life on snooze until your beauty turned on my alarm
I'm willing to give you what I wouldn't give anyone, and that is myself
I am prepared to stay for as long as I have to, even until death
I have thrown ev'ry painful experience away in the trashcan of my memory
When we consummate our love on our honeymoon night, the angels will play
    our symphony
You are the divine words on the pages of my heart, and it is time for you to
    mate me
I am the fish, and you are the hook, bait me
My heart had a condemned sign, and my pain just wouldn't let it mend
I'm learning that if I just let my past go then you my love can come in
There are no mere words to describe you, for your virtue is on love's Best
    Seller's List
I've been waiting patiently to read what's inside, because inside your womb
    is my

TABLE OF CONTENTS!!!

Deep inside the city of her soul lies the table of contents. She is a living epistle. Out of her mouth flows the law of kindness, and out of her belly flows rivers of living water. Inside her fruitful womb are the table of contents to her purpose and destiny. The DNA to her spirit is praise-and-worship which activates the glory of God, which creates an atmosphere where God inhabits the praise of his daughter. The Holy Ghost has revealed to me this woman's table of contents, and since it has been opened up to me, I cannot put her down. I have been reading and studying her contents. Her body of work is impressive, and her volumes are on my Best Seller's List. Because her value is priceless, she has never sold her virtue. Together, people all over the world's relationships will be restored when they read what the Lord has placed in the bookcase of her soul. We have the chemistry of Ossie Davis and Ruby Dee, Ashford and Simpson, Donny Hathaway and Roberta Flack, and Marvin Gaye and Tammi Terrell. We will have *Good Times* like James and Florida Evans without any "temporary layoff, any easy credit ripoff, scratchin'-and-survivin,' or hangin' in a chow line." Destiny, purpose, and favor with God and with man are in her *Table Of Contents*. Husbands, if God reveals to you what's in her table of contents, you will never put her down. You'll always look forward to opening up what's inside of her to read her pages. Let your fingers do the walkin.' Pick up her book and cherish what on the inside of her. Remember… "reading is fundamental".

"MY FAVORITE SUPPER"

I would love for you to spend some time in my personal space
I expect your presence to make a mark that no one can erase
I'll place a welcome mat at the doormat of my heart for you to make your
   humble abode
No one else has the combination to my safe because you are my decode
Because you belong here in my heart, you never have to knock
We will sit on the porch in our golden years, and in our white chairs we will rock
I have cleaned out the old baggage, the residue, and all of my clutter
At some point I've experienced some form a connection but you're intimacy,
   I'll never find another
Your virtue has transformed me, and your love has totally conformed me
I long for your company and companionship, for they're never a bore to me
When I was traveling in the wrong direction, you came to turn my love around
When I was playing hide-and-seek from the real love, you claimed it from the
   lost-and-found
Will you give me the opportunity to fall in love with you?
But I'll wait for you to fall in love so our relationship can include us two
I have prepared a loveseat for you in the living room of my heart
We'll reside in heaven in our studio apartment, and like Siamese twins, we will
   never part
Let's dine on our soul food together without any steroids, preservatives, or
   nitrates
I'll have a buffet of love, and you can climb on my plate
You have soaked up the spills in my life, and like Bounty, you're my heart's
   quicker picker upper
You are my Southern Comfort, and when my soul is famished,
   you are...........

MY FAVORITE SUPPER!!!

I did not plan on writing anything, but this was manna that dropped straight from heaven. I was taking a CEU class on how to massage cancer patients. On day two, before the class started, the instructor, Tracy Walton, led us to a mind-clearing exercise with massage music in the background. As for me, it became so serene that I could feel the presence of the Lord. As a result of focusing on him as the object of my worship, I could hear words resonate in my spirit. I began to write what I heard. After I completed this psalm, I shared it with the class, and they enjoyed it. The original title was *My Last Supper*, but I changed the title. Many people may have known someone, be it a family member, friend, classmate, etc., that had a bout with the Big C. It's an uphill battle to be diagnosed with this dreadful disease and dis-ease, but it's another thing to eat your last supper as your last request! I was likening *The Last Supper* between Christ and his disciples, which was the greatest meal of all time. Whether you are in good health, or have a diagnosis or prognosis, all meals are special. Consequently, my favorite supper will be every meal with my wife and children. Moreover, I will enjoy endlessly the experience with my family and cherish it as if it were my last supper. I will capture the memory of every moment by saying my grace before or after each meal as a sign of infinite gratitude. *Jehovah Jireh* has provided. My cup runneth over. Runneth ends in the suffix, "-eth", and any time a word ends as such, it means a constant and continuous overflow. In other words, my cupboard will never run out, my supply will never end, and my well will never run dry! The favorite meal of the husbands should be his wife's beautiful design. Read between the lines. As Beloved in the Song of Solomon echoes, "Taste my choice fruits." My favorite supper is coming to a bedroom near you and me. AMEN.

"DEPARTMENT OF DEFENSE"

I am your Department of Defense that will provide Homeland Security to your members. I am the Border Patrol to your soul, and I will protect and serve your body, until you come again! My mission is to please you and to make certain that no illegal, demonic immigrants, principalities, powers, rulers of darkness, or any spiritual wickedness in high places trespass against you. I have put on the whole armor of God to quench every fiery dart, scheme, plan, and wile of our enemy. The Lord did not call me to qualify, however, He qualified my call. Before the foundation of the earth, I was anointed, bonafide, certified, deputized, and edified to honor your virtue.

The CEO of the world, El Elyon, has presented me with classified information that can only be used when I say "I Do" and agree with His plans. My answer is, "*Yes Lord*". I've got another "Yes" in my soul. Inside you is purpose and can only come into fruition when we create Destiny's Child when we are joined in Holy Matrimony. I solemnly pledge and vow so to live, that I will be the Chief Champion Lover (CCL) of your body. I am the *Body Police* and you don't have the right to remain silent, because of the *Fire We Make*. Our heterosexual union will never be a Watergate scandal. However, I will chase your water as it falls. As long as Mr. President is inside your Oval Office, you will never impeach me. Our consummation of love making will create a United State of America and the world over.

My badge gives me your body, my night stick is to stick it to you every night. My handcuffs are to arrest and develop your obedience, until you call me Mr. Officer. My belt is to discipline and disciple you. If you are oppositional, you will not resist my arrest. Since I will be the only one to frisk you, I don't need to call for backup, however I will cause you to *Back That Thing Up*! My career is to protect your body and serve you. The question is, *How Do You Like Your Love Served?* *I Stand Accused* of being guilty in the Lover's Court, if there is such a court. Yes, your honor, I am *GUILTY* without and beyond a shadow of reasonable or unreasonable doubt. I am arresting you. I am going downtown to book you and taking you to the 69th Precinct. Why? Because I am the *Body Police*. Assume all positions and spread 'em wide. I am throwing away the key, and will turn my key inside of you to unlock you! The judge has sentenced me not to beg your pardon, though *I Ain't Too Proud To Beg* (and you know it). I'm not going to beg your pardon, but you are going to beg for mercy. Throw yourself on the mercy of the bed, because I have the right to sexually arouse your members. I have been convicted of decent exposure since our bed is undefiled (Hebrews 13:4). I have probable cause to do a strip search because I have been led by the Holy Spirit under the suspicion, that you have been holding contraband. Just for formalities' sake, I will read your Miranda Rights, because you do have a right to a speedy trial. Although I'm not fast, but I am thorough. My speed limit is *Love No Limit*. I don't rush, and because the lovin' ain't going nowhere, I don't have to *Slow Down*.

At any case, I have accepted my lifetime sentence of ecstasy in *Between The Sheets* with you because I'm *Livin' For The Love Of You*. I do solemnly pledge before God, Indivisible, who has already granted justice for heterosexual couples to say...*I Do...., But To Who*?!

Printed in the United States
By Bookmasters